MW00355536

Mañana
Starts *Today*

*Affirmations to Jumpstart
Your Heart, Mind, and Soul*

Sandra Elaine Scott

MAÑANA STARTS TODAY Affirmations to Jumpstart Your Heart, Mind, and Soul

PUBLISHED BY VISION YOUR DREAMS
www.visionyourdreamspublishing.com

PRINTED IN THE UNITED STATES OF AMERICA

The author of the book does not dispense, recommend or prescribe advice, activities or the use of any technique as a form of treatment for a physical, emotional or medical problem. The intent of the author is only to offer information of a general nature to help you in your quest for emotional and spiritual well-being. The information presented here—as with any outside information—should be viewed as seed material for contemplation only. In the event you use any of the information in this book for yourself, which is your constitutional right, the author and the publisher assume no responsibility for your actions.

Library of Congress Control Number: 2013922317

ISBN-10: 0615924468

ISBN-13: 978-0-615-92446-5

Author's photograph ~ Tracey Harper

Cover Art & Book Illustrator ~ Jean Maniscalco

Book Design & Layout ~ Karen White

Visit website at: www.mananastartstoday.com

This book is dedicated to
all the dreamers who
turn their someday
into today.

Wishing You
Inspired
Today

Jade

Table of Contents

Table of Contents

Introduction

This book is a collection of affirmations designed to assist you in moving forward on your goals and dreams.

Your goals and dreams manifest when you do things today. Most people put off what they want while waiting...Waiting for the economy. Waiting for children to grow up. Waiting to get that degree. Waiting to take a step. And while they wait, time marches on...Time is spent waiting for tomorrow. But the world moves on. The earth continues to spin on its axis, the sun rises and sets, the water ebbs and flows, and dreams and goals remain unrealized.

Mañana Starts Today. Today your dreams are waiting for you to act. As the sun rises so do your dreams...So today...Get moving. Today take action, because your dreams will not wait another second.

Mañana Starts Today! Today, turn to the divine, ask for guidance. God is waiting for you to live your life to the fullest. Mañana Starts Today! Today listen to your heart. Your spirit is waiting for you to guide your way. Mañana Starts Today! Today engage your mind; it is waiting to lead you into action.

You will find affirmations in this book that are heart-, mind-, and soul-centered. Each of the 49 affirmations offers suggestions intended to expand your thinking and jumpstart your day. There are many ways to use these affirmations. You may choose to pick an affirmation daily, at random, or even choose one for an entire week. It takes courage and faith to jumpstart your life. Reciting an affirmation helps to give breath and life to the depth of your dreams.

You can do it...*Mañana Starts Today!*

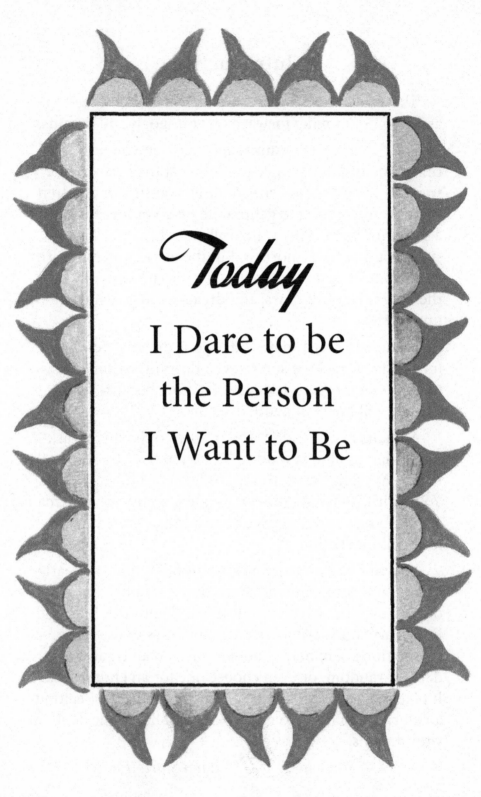

Today

I Dare to be the Person I Want to Be

Today is the day to live your authentic self, no apologies, and no excuses to anyone. Today, dare to be exceptional. Today, feed the urge of your desires and give voice to the thoughts and aspirations of your innermost soul.

On this day, say YES to what you want and silence the negative energy and thoughts around you. Stake a claim on your life and the power of yes.

Today is the day to claim your power. Be the person you want from the core of your being. Show up as yourself today. The world is waiting for you.

Today I dare to be the person I want to be

" He who knows others is wise. He who knows himself is enlightened."

~ Lao Tzu

Today

I Love Myself
Unconditionally

Today, hug yourself and love the person you are. When we are in love, we throw ourselves wholeheartedly into the new relationship. We tell everyone we know about the one we love. We are giddy; we smile a lot and we are joyous.

Today, you are charged with being in love with YOU! Talk about yourself with the same joy and abandonment that you would talk about another. Walk around with your head held high, as you are a person with a secret love. Take pride and ownership of loving yourself unconditionally. Today you are a Man/Woman in love.

Yes, you love yourself unconditionally and the world today loves you back. Embrace that love and walk joyfully into the day.

Today I love myself unconditionally

" Love yourself first and everything else falls into line. You really have to love yourself to get anything done in this world."

~ Lucille Ball

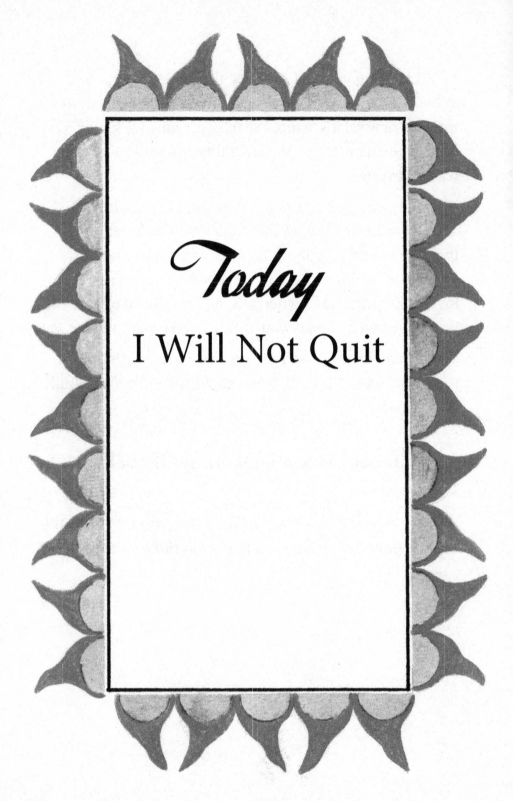

Today

I Will Not Quit

Today, no matter what, give it your all! Especially when the way seems daunting, ***do not quit***. The last person who completes the race is still in the race because he crosses the finish line.

The race of life awaits you today. Don't give up no matter what. It is easy to say "it's too hard, the road is long," etc. It is more rewarding to keep on moving and not sit down midway. The race is neither for the swift nor the strong but the one who endures.

On this day, go with gusto and repeat the mantra "I will not quit no matter what." On your journey, you may encounter naysayers, who may use their negativity to disarm you with killer phrases such as "be realistic, that'll never work," or any other negative belief that holds "false" for them.

Today, you have the right to tune those voices out and do what holds true for you. Create the okay chorus in your mind, and think and say over and over; "I will not give up."

Today I will not quit

" If you live long enough, you'll make mistakes. But if you learn from them, you'll be a better person. It's how you handle adversity, not how it affects you. The main thing is never quit, never quit, never quit."

~ William J. Clinton

Today

I Shine

Today you are filled with light and air. Shine and let the whole world see the sparkle in your eyes, heart, and mind. Today is the day to celebrate your spirit, your light, and your truth. Let that brilliant radiant beam shine so that others may see their own true worth through you.

As you light up the planet with your brilliance, new opportunities and people will cross your path. Just like the stars that light the night sky, so do you light the way for others to see their own path. Believe in the power of your light. So that when the going gets tough, even the smallest glow will help you to keep moving forward.

Raise your vibration today. Shine highly and intently with love in your heart and it will be reflected back to you.

Today I shine

" And as we let our own light shine, we unconsciously give other people permission to do the same."

~ Nelson Mandela

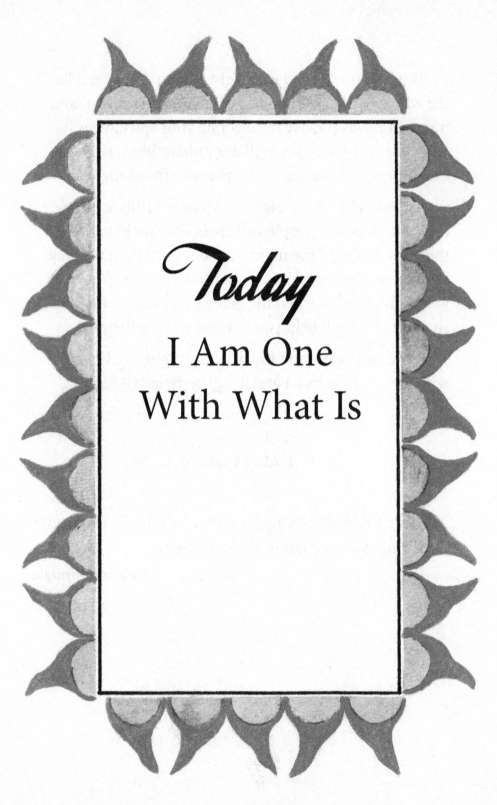

Today

I Am One
With What Is

Today is the day to be in harmony with the Universe. Share in God's creation today and join in a vibrant celebration of life.

Today, be in perfect peace with the world. There is no separation, no anxiety; today is a day entwined within the chords of love. Feel the calming presence of this love and call on it throughout the day.

Today be attuned with the Spirit and let that be the navigator for your day, accepting a role today in God's master design for the Universe. In your harmonious acceptance of what is, you allow the universe to just be and you are better for it.

Today treat everyone you meet as an extension of you and an extension of God. Treat them gently with kind and loving care, as we all are one.

Today I am one with what is

" He who lives in harmony with himself lives in harmony with the universe."

~ Marcus Aurelius

Today

My Mind
is Focused

Today you are focused on what you want. Your mind is clear on your goals. You know with a single-minded purpose what you need to do to succeed.

Today your mind does not waver from its course. To focus is to pay attention. When you have clarity of your purpose, it helps to keep you on course and focused on your outcome.

Today your mind is sharp and with crystal clear determination. Focus on your goals with positive outcomes.

Today my mind is focused

" Concentrate all your thoughts upon the work at hand. The sun's rays do not burn until brought to a focus."
~ Alexander Graham Bell

Today

I Laugh

Today make it all about laughing. Laughing is an essential ingredient to being less stressed. Have you ever laughed just for the joy of laughing aloud? Today do that. Laugh out loud.

Open the laugh lines to your heart and soul and take pleasure in the silly and the fun today. Recall a time in your life when you acted silly; now go back and laugh real loud.

Belly-laugh from your gut. Laugh until your stomach hurts because you have not used your laugh muscle. If you feel silly doing it, you are doing it just right. If you need more inspiration, listen to any recording of a baby laughing. That alone is guaranteed to put a smile on your face. Call someone and tell him or her a silly joke. Watch a comedy and laugh. Do anything that will make you laugh out loud today.

Need a little inspiration? Try a knock-knock joke. Here's a silly one to get you off to a fun start.

> Knock knock.
> Who's there?
> Doris.
> Doris who?
> Doris locked, that's why I'm knocking!

Today I laugh

" A good laugh is sunshine in the house."
>   *~ William Makepeace Thackeray*

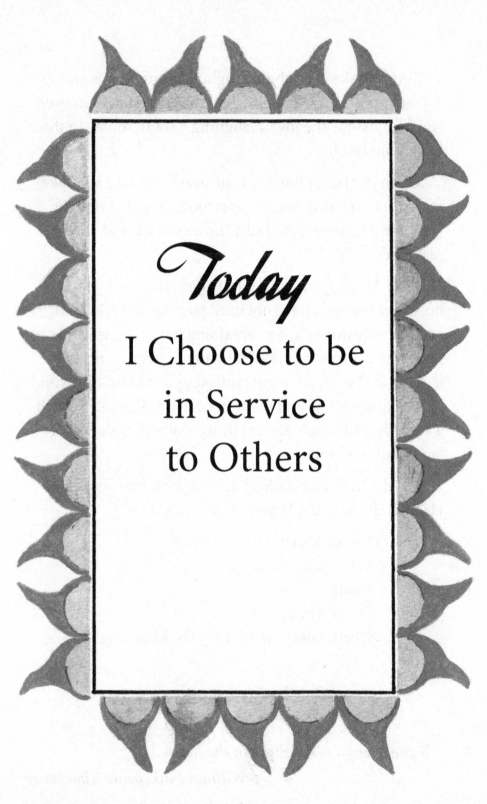

Today

I Choose to be in Service to Others

Today, think outside yourself and be of service to others. Today, ask others how you may help them and what is it that they may need to help them live an inspired life.

Today you are called upon to be a transformational agent; be brave enough to be in service and give of your heart. On this day, make a difference in your own life and others. When you see the world through love-colored eyes, the world's reflection of love will be illuminated ten-fold.

Today do your part to help those in need. Count your blessings for what you have, for even if to you it may seem little…to others you may have much. For within your ability to do what you are able to do, you will transform a piece of the planet from me to we.

You get to choose how you want to show up in the world. Leave the world a better place and leave behind the legacy of love.

Today I choose to be in service to others

" *I may be here for a short while, gone tomorrow into oblivion or until the days come to take me away. But, in whatever part you play, be remembered as part of a legacy…of sharing dreams and changing humanity for the better. It's that legacy that never dies.*"

~ Author Unknown

Today

I Seek Out New Opportunities

Today, create an opportunity for something new and different. As you work on your goals and dreams, explore every opportunity, as you never know when you will be motivated to take a chance and leap into something new.

The opportunities today may appear as a new thought, inspired action, or even a chance encounter as you walk down the street. Limitless possibilities open up when you allow yourself to be receptive to chance. You never know when the Universe is conspiring in your favor, so treat all moments as precious commodities towards your goals.

Be fortuitous and greet each moment as life's good fortune smiling upon you. God's time is always favorable, so trust in that knowledge and freely accept these moments of grace in your life.

Today I seek out new opportunities

" Every single moment of our lives, whether borne of joy or pain, has the potential for grace realized. Whether it's an opportunity to learn something, or an unexpected connection made, or finding love where you thought none existed. Those are the gifts from God!"

~ Rosalind Cash

Today
I Trust Myself

Today is the day to trust in your gut. Trust within every fiber of your being that you know the right thing to do. You know the right step. With every decision you make today, be confident in the outcome as you rely on yourself.

It matters not today what outsiders think; in your heart, you know what is right for you. Drop into that place of being within yourself. And without question, know you are in control, and because you are in control and know the truth, trust yourself.

Today you must trust in that quiet place at the center of your being. Today you do not need validation from anyone but you. Trust the process, trust your mind, trust your soul, and trust yourself!

Today I trust myself

" *Trust yourself. Create the kind of self that you will be happy to live with all your life. Make the most of yourself by fanning the tiny, inner sparks of possibility into flames of achievement.*"

~ *Golda Meir*

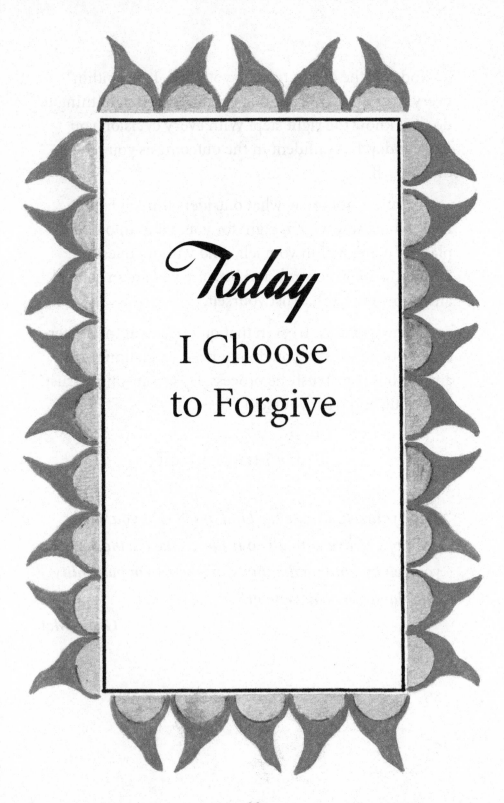

Today

I Choose
to Forgive

Today, make the conscious decision to release the negative toxins in your mind and forgive. Whether the person who needs forgiving is you or the need is to forgive another, today is the day to be free of judgment, loss, and pain and simply forgive.

The choice is yours today. Even if people have emotionally hurt you, they have no power over you if you do not give it to them. Ironically, one of the Greek definitions for forgiveness is "let go."

Are you holding a grudge against someone, or has someone hurt you and you find it hard to forgive them? The true power of forgiveness is an example of divine mercy. On this day, give yourself the gift of grace and compassion. Today you are encouraged to LET IT GO! Have a joyous day and forgive!

Today I choose to forgive

" The weak can never forgive. Forgiveness is the attribute of the strong."

~ *Mahatma Gandhi*

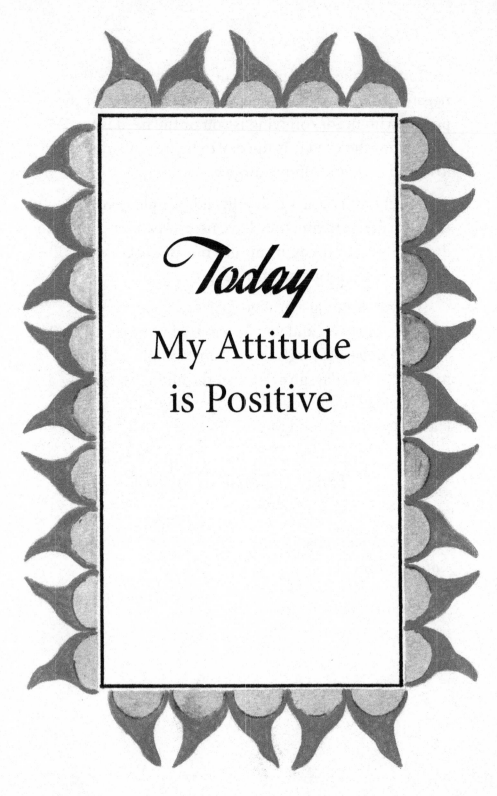

Today
My Attitude
is Positive

Today you will view the world around you from a position of positivity. With this perspective, the glass is neither half-empty nor half-full. Your outlook today is so positive you see it as a full glass with air and liquid.

Today, focus that positive energy on all that you have. If you feel that you have little, appreciate even that, as you have more than those who have none. Your outlook today starts with the ability to take a breath acknowledging that you are a living contributor to this planet.

Today, be optimistic and you will be able to confidently approach any situation. Today the world is smiling upon your sunny disposition. In turn, your positive outlook will influence everyone you meet today.

Today my attitude is positive

" Our attitude toward life determines life's attitude towards us."

~ Earl Nightingale

Today

I Stand in My Truth

Today is your day to stand tall and proud in your authentic self. Today you get to be YOU! That means no kowtowing to others, no bending your will. Today you have a backbone and stand tall in your truth.

As you greet the world on this day, you stand erect and proud of who you are. Today there is no blaming or apologizing for being you. People will see the real you as you stand up in your space and claim who you are.

Today claim the truth that you are a unique being, capable of bringing your authentic self to those who are touched by your presence. This is your day. Own it, claim it, and stand in it.

Today I stand in my truth

"Get up, stand up, Stand up for your rights. Get up, stand up, Don't give up the fight."

~ Bob Marley

Today

I Inspire Joy

Be joyful today. Today you are charged with spreading this joy throughout your being. When you are completely overflowing with joy, run out and share it with the world.

It pays to be joyous as it is an infectious state of being. When you are filled with joy people will stop and ask, "Why are you so cheerful?" You can give them any reason. If you need one, try this…"I love my life and it's good to be alive!"

This sumptuous answer is usually so unexpected that it may take people aback. Nevertheless, you will have connected to a piece of their soul and be able to connect with them.

Give yourself and others this precious gift today. There is, shall we say, "joy" in the giving and receiving of joy. Be that person of inspiration. It costs nothing and gives so much back to the world.

Today I Inspire joy

" Joy is increased by spreading it to others"
                                    ~ Robert Murray McCheyne

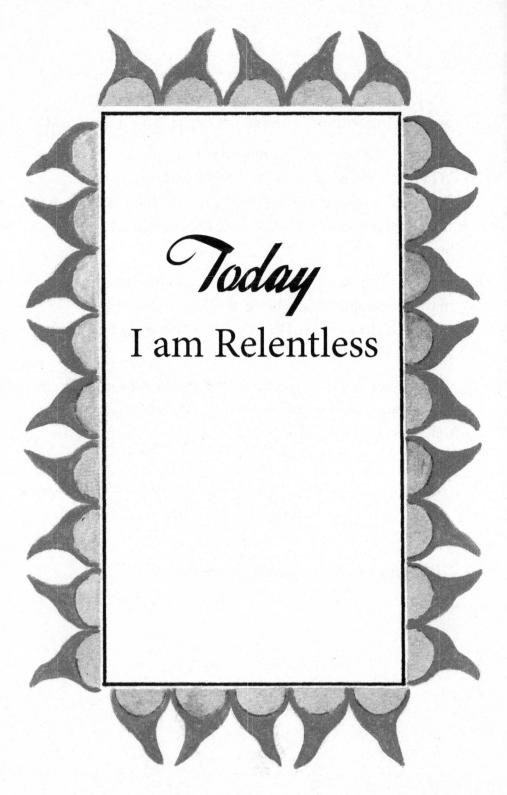

Today

I am Relentless

Today you are relentless. You are fearless and you pursue your goals with a determination of spirit. To be relentless means to be unyielding. Therefore do not slow down for anyone. Keep after your goal. Do not stop under any circumstances, even if it means you have to tug and pull; haul yourself to your personal finish line.

Ask yourself: Is there a new adventure, a new goal, that you dare to try? Take a chance of self-discovery and ask "why not?" What risks have you taken? The risk of life is in living and being fully present. Like a dog with a bone, hold on to that passion. Keep at it. If it is someone you need to call, keep calling. If it is someone you need to email, do it now. Today, just go for it. You are relentless!

Today I am relentless

" There have been so many people who have said to me, "You can't do that," but I've had an innate belief that they were wrong. Be unwavering and relentless in your approach."

~ Halle Berry

Today

I am Beautiful

Today, acknowledge the beauty of who you are. Rely on your senses to see, touch, and smell your beauty. You are beautiful inside and out. So today, accept your beauty by treating yourself as a beautiful child of God

The true beauty of self lies within each of us. Each day, look at yourself in the mirror and reflect on the beauty of your spirit. When you recognize your own beauty, your own specialness, others too will see you as the gorgeous, precious specimen of humanity that you are.

Smile gorgeous! Today this affirmation should translate in all that you do and give your gift of beauty to the world.

Today I am beautiful

"Beauty is not in the face; beauty is a light in the heart. "
~ Kahlil Gibran

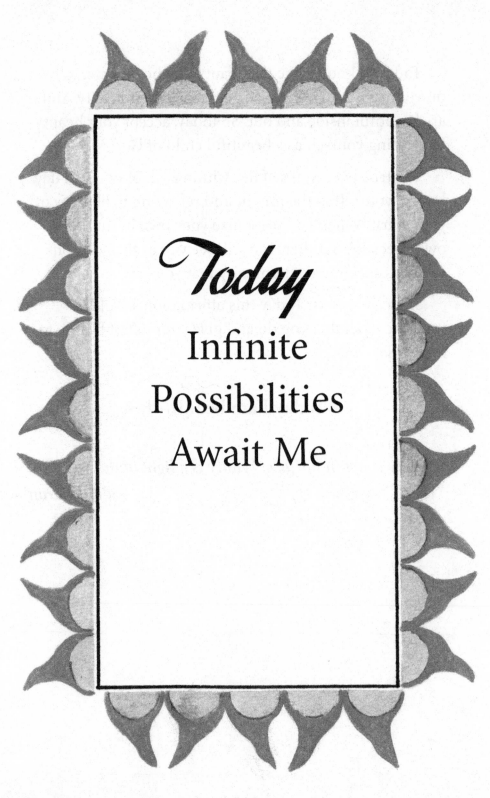

Today

Infinite
Possibilities
Await Me

Today is your day to open your eyes to the unforeseen and imagine the day with infinite possibilities. When your mind is awakened, you are able to see things you would never have imagined.

Today, look around you and keep your eyes open for the unexpected. Use every moment and be on the alert for the promise the new day brings!

As surely as the sun rises today, so does the potential of something new rise up to meet you. And when nightfall comes, listen to the quiet and hitch your dreams and goals to those stars. As you lift your eyes to the heavens, your dreams are shining as brightly in your mind as they were in the dawn.

As countless as the stars in the sky, so are your hopes and dreams, they are limitless, bound only by your imagination. With every breath you take, see your possibilities as endless. Today just go for it.

Today Infinite Possibilities await me

" Without leaps of imagination, or dreaming, we lose the excitement of possibilities. Dreaming, after all, is a form of planning."

~ Gloria Steinem

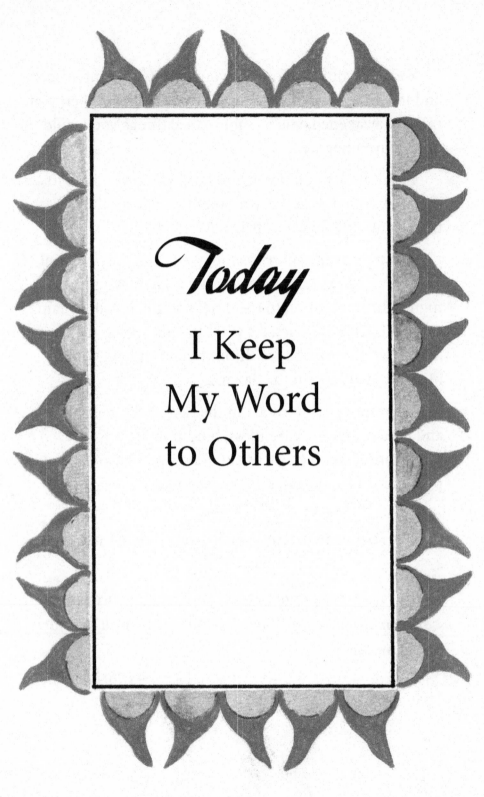

Today

I Keep
My Word
to Others

Today, keep your word. When you give your word, there is an easy temptation to say "forget about it," or "never mind." Only make commitments you can realistically keep. This may mean a harsh reality of saying no to others without reservation or hesitation but with preservation of your word. Once given, keep your word; do not take it lightly.

We are so often ready to avoid disappointing others that we say yes to the mundane and then break the promise because we really didn't mean it to begin with. Today create a new habit. Only commit to what you really know in your heart is true and then keep your word. Make your word today feel like glue on your tongue. If you say it, you believe it, you act on it, and then you do it!

Today your word is your bond. Keep it and you become a person of integrity. Your word is your word. Therefore, figure out how committed you are today to keeping it.

Today I keep my word to others

" I will not violate my covenant or alter the word that went forth from my lips."

~ Psalm 89:34

Today

I Prosper

Today you are aware of the abundance in your life. Prosperity is often measured by the dollars in a bank account. Today you are aware that to be prosperous is so much more.

The way to acknowledge your prosperity is to embrace your ability to breathe, pursue your dreams and to keep the mindset to live each day to its fullest. Give thanks to the Universe for your abundance.

Today, bless everything that you touch and everyone you encounter and share the feeling of prosperity and abundance. This simple blessing does not cost you anything and spreads the universal message that there is enough for all.

Today you are indeed prosperous. As your cup of abundance overflows, give thanks and praise.

Today I prosper

" All that is mine by Divine Right is now released and reaches me in great avalanches of abundance, under grace in miraculous ways. "

~ *Florence Scovel Shinn*

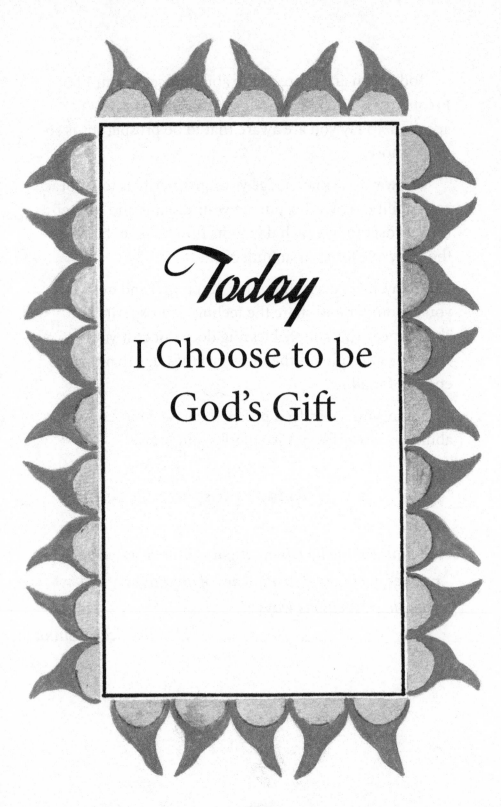

Today

I Choose to be
God's Gift

Today is the day you activate your gifts. God made you special, and today is your day to share your unique self with the world.

Have you wondered about the gifts that God has given you? Do you honor your spirit and share these gifts with others? Perhaps you have the gift of laughter, the gift of comfort, the gift of joy, the gift of sharing, the gift of truth, the gift of friendship. Whatever your gift, you are commanded to share it with others so that the world may fully experience the wonder that is you.

Today is your day; choose to be God's gift and use your gifts, spread your wings, and let those around you know that you honor them by sharing a bit of yourself.

Today I choose to be God's gift

" When you are not sharing your gifts with the world, you are causing suffering in the world. Someone who needs your specific gift is not being served."

~ Adam Markel

Today

I Scream
My Dream
Out Loud

Today is the day to share your dream with the world. Look in the mirror and scream it as loud as you can. Imprint that dream into your vocal cords and your brain and get ready to share it with the world.

Whispering your dream is not an option. This is the day to proudly scream your dream to every person that you encounter. Treat this moment like the day you first fell in love, and let everyone know that you have a dream and you are proud of it.

On this day, proclaim your dream to everyone who is within earshot and even those who are far away. Pick up the phone, send an email, drop a post card, whatever works for you, just do it!

You will be amazed today that when you scream your dream out loud, the Universe will shout back answers with people, thoughts, and inspirations to help you manifest your dream.

Today I scream my dream out loud

" Stand upright, speak thy thoughts, declare the truth thou hast, that all may share; be bold, proclaim it everywhere: They only live who dare."

~ Voltaire

Today
I am Grateful

Today be grateful for every millisecond. Begin your day by saying "thank you" for waking up this morning. Give thanks that as the sun rose, so shall you rise up to meet the new day.

When you say thank you first thing, you immediately access the joy to jumpstart your day and have the first thing to be grateful for. You also now have something to be grateful for at the end of the day when you lie down to go to sleep.

Today, create a space in your mind and dedicate it as your "thank you" closet. As occurrences happen throughout your day, take a moment, say thank you, and tuck it in to the "thank you" closet.

You will be surprised when you peek in that closet at the end of the day everything will spill out, and you will be overwhelmed with the number of things you had to be grateful for on this day.

Today I am grateful

" *A single grateful thought toward heaven is the most perfect prayer.*"

~ Gotthold Ephraim Lessing

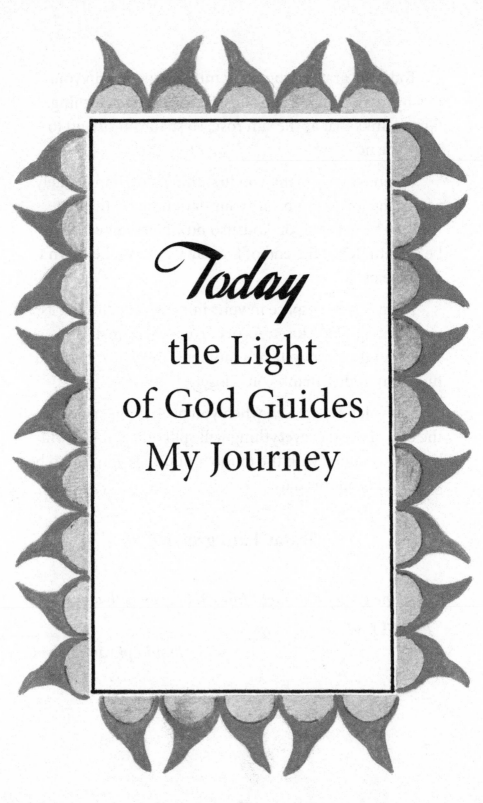

Today
the Light
of God Guides
My Journey

Today is the day to seek guidance from God. Ask God to continually light your path and then follow in a positive direction. On days when the journey seems endless and you are not sure what path to take, ask God to light the way.

If at times you feel that negative energy has taken your light, you only have to remember that water may be able to douse a flame but God's eternal light will always be within you to guide your way.

Take heart in knowing that you are never alone on this quest called life and that you can easily call upon the light at any time. You are a child of God; rest assured that your way is ordained and paved with an eternal light.

Today the light of God guides my journey

" You are my lamp, O LORD; the LORD turns my darkness into light."

~ 2 Samuel 22:29

Today

I am Creative

This is your day to tap into your inner being. Today "think outside the proverbial box" and become wildly creative. Discover that place within you that is resourceful, is fun and imaginative, and let your inner child out to inspire your day.

When you are inspired, you release the mental and physical blocks that may have kept you from moving forward on your goals. Today, be an inspiration to others as you unleash your creativity into the world.

Today there is no such thing as a bad idea. No criticism is allowed. Take gigantic risks, and let free thought reign supreme. Your ideas are the keys to manifesting your dream life. Today, turn your creative thoughts into tangible ideas. Turn these ideas into reality so that you inspire others and make a difference in the world.

Today I am creative

" Creativity is contagious, pass it on."

~ Albert Einstein

Today

My Body
is Perfect

Today you see yourself as a perfect expression of God. As God's work is perfect, therefore you are perfect. Today you see no blemishes, no flaws, no illness, and no wrong. Today, you understand that your body is a shining being of God's perfection.

Just for today, embody yourself as perfection. Our society has trained us to be misinformed about who we are. We tend to find fault within ourselves and look to fix what the Divine has created. The definition of perfect is conforming absolutely to the description or definition of an ideal type. That ideal type today is you.

Stand in your essence, proud of your being, of who you are. When you are out and about in your world today, view it through perfect eyes. Look in the mirror, and dance and shout to the tune of your own perfect being.

Give thanks to your body parts. Smile and lovingly accept each body part as an authentic expression of the Divine. Today you really are perfect.

Today my body is perfect

" I praise you because I am fearfully and wonderfully made; your works are wonderful, I know that full well.

~ Psalm 139:1

Today

I Trust in God's Plan for Me

Today is the day to completely put your faith in God and trust. Allow yourself to fully trust in God. This trust will help to give you the confidence that everything will be okay. Faith and trust go hand in hand.

When you have absolute trust, you put your fate and faith in God's hand and hold hands in a co-created mutual relationship of love. The relationship that you create today is based on respect that there is something greater than you in the world. With this knowing, it gives you the yes mentality to meet the day.

As you start your day…Say "Yes I trust." Take the "yes but" tendency out of your vocabulary today. Saying "but" is just another symptom of not having the faith to just trust. With trust, there is no fear as you move with anticipation and hope for God's plan as it unfolds today.

Today I trust in God's plan for me

" *Commit thy way unto the LORD; trust also in him; and he shall bring it to pass.*"

~ Psalm 37:5

Today

I Ask for Help

Today ask for help. Asking for help conveys that you are strong and you are not alone. Today you understand that it is okay to rely on those who can help you with your goals, your dreams, or even just general support.

Realize that some people will look at you and just say no. You are okay with that no, as that no moves you forward. No just moves you closer to the person who can say yes to you and allows you to explore other options and to ask again.

If you have a particular need, you must ask, and keep on asking until you get the help you seek. After all, what is the best that could happen, that person may just say YES!

Today I ask for help

" Blessed are those who can give without remembering and take without forgetting."

~ *Elizabeth Bibesco*

Today

I Smile

Today your smile radiates for the world to see. It takes only seventeen muscles to smile. A smile changes your countenance and will give the outlook of your day a much-needed facelift.

If you have not smiled in a while, stand in the mirror and practice. As you smile, your body will relax, and your being will be transformed. This transformation will boost your confidence and give you energy for your day.

Your smile is the entry point to make a difference to someone else without saying a word. Smile and the world will smile back at you. The world is waiting for your smile. Show up and smile brightly today.

Today I smile

" *Every time you smile at someone, it is an action of love, a gift to that person, a beautiful thing.*"

~ *Mother Teresa*

Today
I Create
Magical
Moments

Today magic is in the air. And, guess what? It's your magic! Everywhere you go today feel that spark of creativity, ingenuity and the wonderful burst of energy of just being alive.

Today the power is within you and you can bestow your magic upon others. Feel the strength of who you are. Rather than waiting for miracles to happen today, become the miracle and let the magic flow from your being.

As you tend your business today, discover the places where you can tap into that magic and create, be, and do. Magical moments happen when you allow the Universe to conspire with you. Be exuberant in your being, be magical, and celebrate life.

Today I create magical moments

" Magic is believing in yourself, if you can do that, you can make anything happen."

~ Johann Wolfgang von Goethe

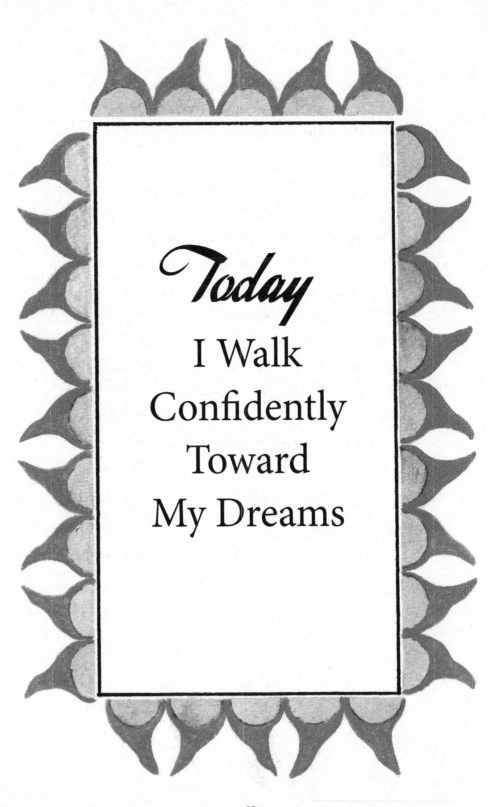

Today
I Walk
Confidently
Toward
My Dreams

Today you are confident and clear about your dreams and goals. On this day, you're able to easily articulate your dream to others and begin to turn your vision into reality. With this assurance, you know that the clearer you are about your dream, the easier it will be to share it with others.

The ability to be confident will give you the momentum to move forward. Your confidence is also essential when asking for help and gaining support from others for your goals. You easily strut like a peacock when you have faith in yourself and your ability to manifest the life of your dreams.

Even if it is hard for others to see your vision, hold that vision close to your heart and keep putting one foot in front of the other. Today, walk with purpose and be assured that with clarity and confidence your dreams are waiting for you to fulfill them.

Today I walk confidently toward my dreams

" Go confidently in the direction of your dreams. Live the life you have imagined."

~ Henry David Thoreau

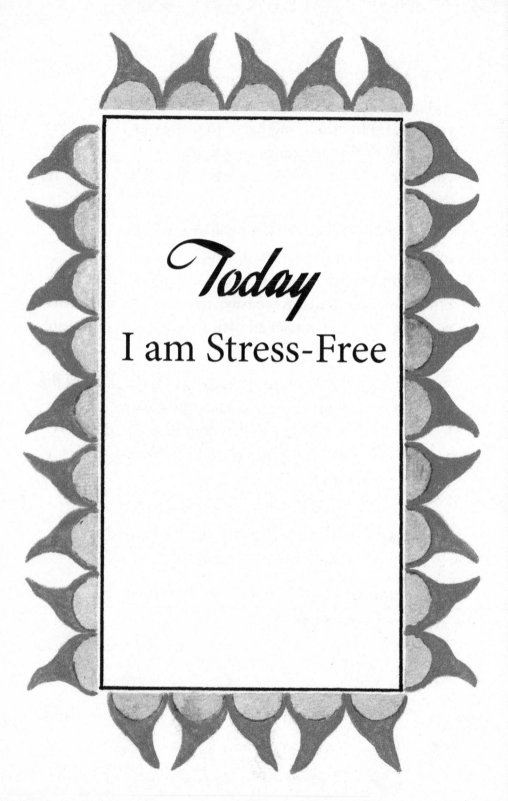

Today

I am Stress-Free

Today you walk through your day unencumbered by stress. Today, reframe all thoughts in your head to be stress free and without prejudice to yourself.

There are three types of stress triggers. They are accidental hassles, major life changes, and ongoing problems. These triggers often are the pressures or the boiling points that keep us from living a harmonious life.

An example of the first trigger, an accidental hassle, would be a flat tire. Yes, it might make you late, you might have to breathe deeply, but trust in the fact that there is nothing to be worried about or to agitate your heart. The second stress trigger would be major life changes (e.g., death, birth) in the circle of life; those are storms and starbursts to be acknowledged and kept in perspective. The third stressor is ongoing issues. This form of stress is continual and while a drop at a time may do little outside damage, over time can erode your inner being. Bills, work, yes they will always be there, so handle them. Breathe in and out and go with the flow of your life.

Today, lean into life with the attitude that absolutely nothing is going to stress you out. Breathe in, exhale, and walk into the day less stressed.

Today I am stress-free

" Stressed spelled backwards is desserts. Coincidence? I think not!"

~ Author Unknown

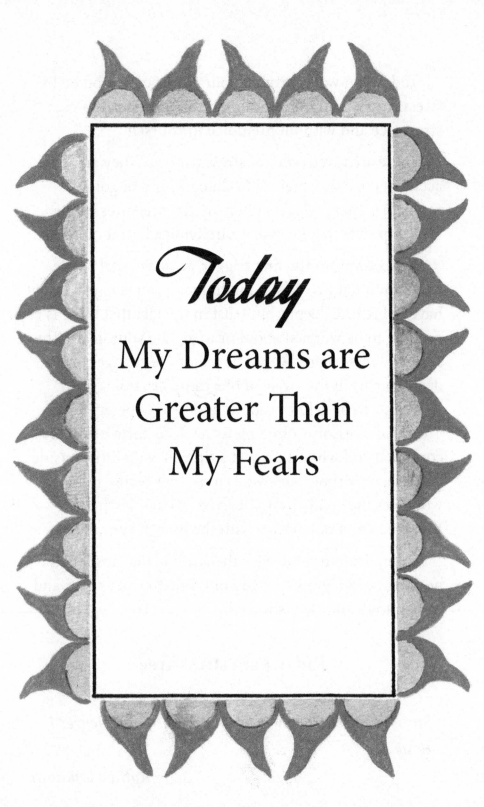

Today

My Dreams are Greater Than My Fears

Today, live in faith that all your dreams are coming true. Today you know that faith and fear cannot coexist at the same time, so today you choose to live in faith.

When you emphatically believe that there is a force greater than you and that God is a collaborator in all your endeavors, you are able to live in faith.

Faith is electric and alive whereas fear is static. Faith is all about movement. You move when you have faith. You move to take action. When you are committed to your dreams and have faith, you are able to make conscious choices to aid in your success. So dream big today and without fear.

Today is your day to play, to win, live large, and dream on a grand scale. Set your dreams in motion today because today you live in faith.

Today my dreams are greater than my fears

" The LORD is my light and my salvation; Whom shall I fear? The LORD is the strength of my life; Of whom shall I be afraid?"

~ Psalm 27:1

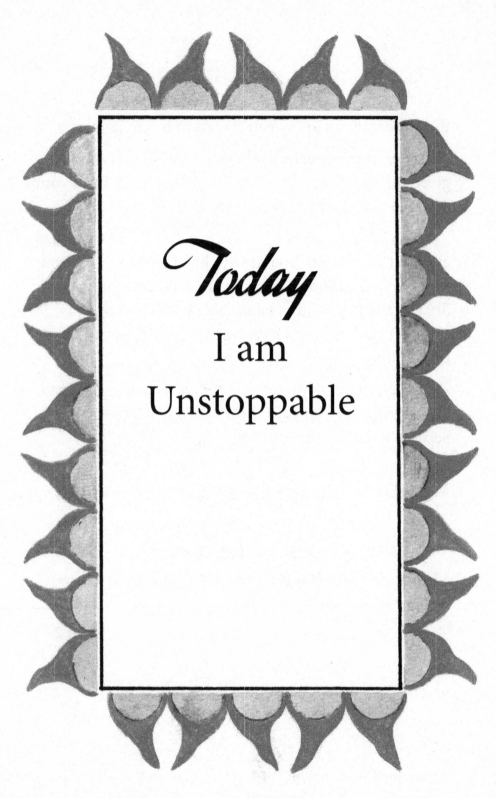

Today

I am
Unstoppable

Today, nothing stands in your way. You have hit the green light for every road you want to take.

You are unstoppable! Today you will push through all barriers, and no is not an option. As you go through your day, break through the chains of can not, will not, and impossible. Just keep moving forward.

On this day, own your greatness. Harness your power and it will give you strength to move. Make the commitment today to take action in your life with the self-awareness that you are indeed unstoppable.

There is no obstacle in your path but you. Let the history of your yesterdays be your motivation for your todays. Need a little help? Use this guided imagery "that like the tides of the ocean you are a person in movement and in flow."

Today I am unstoppable

" Life takes on meaning when you become motivated, set goals and charge after them in an unstoppable manner."
~ Les Brown

Today

I am Bold

Today be bold and outrageous in your thoughts, your choices, and your deeds. Walk a little cocky and know without any doubt that it pays to be bold.

Today it's okay to break the rules of propriety. Say yes to the inner you that is daring and audacious. Brag a little today and be a little flashy as you share your dreams and goals. Walk around as if you have the biggest secret in the world and you are going to spill it.

Your resolution today is to be bold enough to act as if you are on the adventure of a lifetime. You are indeed the captain of your fate, so play it up today and have fun with it.

Today I am bold

" The way of the superior person is threefold; virtuous, they are free from anxieties; wise they are free from perplexities; and bold they are free from fear."

~ Confucius

Today

I Embrace Life

Life is to be enjoyed. Today, live each moment and embrace your existence on this planet. Use your five senses to make sense of who you are.

What is it that you see today? What smells are around you; are they flowery pungent, or clean and crisp? What is it that you hear? Are they the sounds of the birds, traffic horns, or the sounds of silence? What is nourishing you? How does it taste? Is it sweet, bitter, sour, or even fiery hot? What can you feel? When you touch it, is it soft and supple or is hard and rough? If one or more of your senses are missing, other senses are magnified, so be grateful for the ability that your other senses have compensated.

Embrace life today, embrace Spirit for giving it to you. Walk around feeling really entitled and a blessed being on this planet. You deserve to be here, and as you have life and you breathe, so do you exist.

Today I embrace life

" You are a child of the universe, no less than the trees and the stars; you have a right to be here. And whether or not it is clear to you, no doubt the universe is unfolding as it should."

~ Max Erhmann

Today

I Defy Any Challenge

Today, be present and engage in life. Rise up to meet any challenges that may come your way. Today, will yourself to do better and to be better than ever before.

Your way is made plain when you walk through a challenge rather than avoid it. You are so confident today that you can take the world on and the world steps aside and lets you through.

On this day, defy any obstacles that are in your path. With this conviction, your disposition is positive and has the strength to overcome any obstacle. When you see an obstacle, kick it aside or resolve it on the spot and keep on moving.

Today is your day to be the superhero in your life. You have the power of heart, mind and soul to conquer any situation, and thrive.

Today I defy any challenge

" *The phoenix hope can wing her way through the desert skies, and still defying fortune's spite; revive from ashes and rise.*"

~ Miguel de Cervantes Saavedra

Today

I am Free

Today you are no longer enslaved to what doesn't serve you. You are free to be, to think, to do. You have a freedom of expression today that is uniquely and solely yours.

When you choose to let go of others thoughts about you, and walk around free of self-doubt, stress, or worry, you are liberated.

Today it is your choice to be free. So what does that mean? It means you can sing as loudly as you want even if it's out of tune, you can dance to the beat of your own drum; you can live your life in the throes of your own passion and not the dictates of someone else. To be truly free today, you must embrace every decision you make, every road you walk on your own freedom journey.

Today I am free.

" To be free and to live a free life—that is the most beautiful thing there is."

~ Miguel Indurain

Today

My Faith Lets Me Leap

Today, look up, have absolute faith, and jump. The truth is that everyone looks down when they are jumping, figuratively or literally. Figuratively, people pray for something or someone to catch them. Literally, people look down to see if there is a net below or, how far the jump is, or if the safety harness is secure.

Today you jump head first towards your goals and dreams without checking all the angles.

On this day, just leap knowing that your faith will carry you on your journey. Nothing good comes from looking down. So look up and with faith, leap.

Today, choose to have faith in the process, to have faith in who you are, and to have faith in your abilities. Simply put, have faith, and leap!

Today my faith lets me leap

" The artist never entirely knows. We guess. We may be wrong, but we take leap after leap in the dark."

~ *Agnes de Mille*

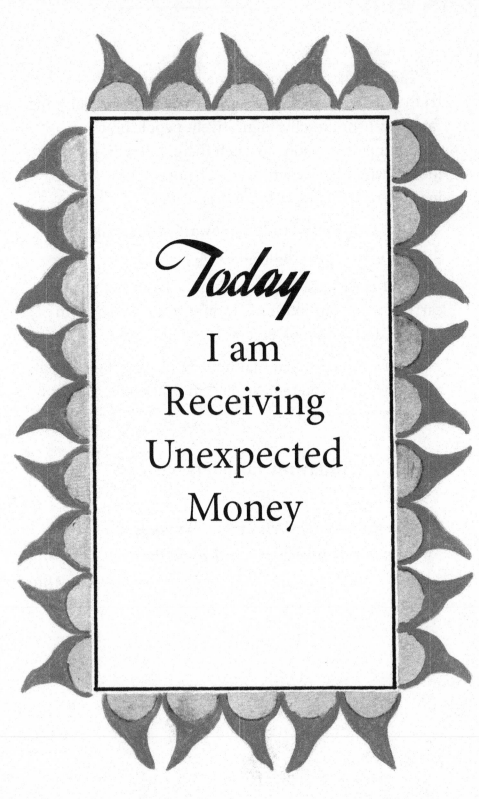

Today
I am
Receiving
Unexpected
Money

Today, open your eyes, heart, and ears to new possibilities for increasing your financial abundance. The universal truth of money is that it is energy. As the sun rises today, adjust your financial vibration by shifting your mindset. You will be amazed that the energy of money is flowing and is waiting for you.

Today, first say thank you to the Universe for the income you have, that you have spent, and income that is yet to come. Unexpected money is attainable when you open your mind to new possibilities. As you go about your day, it may come from an inspired thought to call someone who may be able to put you in touch with a new resource or meditating for a positive flow of wealth.

As you focus today on creating positive income streams allow this moment to be a space of gratitude for all that you have, of what you will receive, and for what you will make of it.

Today I am receiving unexpected money

" But remember the Lord your God, for it is he who gives you the ability to produce wealth, and so confirms his covenant, which he swore to your ancestors, as it is today."

~ Deuteronomy 8:18

Today

I Honor
My Word
to Myself

Today everything that you said you would do tomorrow, do now. Mañana Starts Today! We often lie to ourselves and say we will do something (e.g., start a new diet, seek a new job, find a mate). Well, today is that day to honor your word.

Take action and do it now! The tendency in life is to keep our word to others but not honor commitments to ourselves. Today honor your word to yourself. You are the most important person in your life so respect that and keep your word to yourself today. You will have the utmost integrity with yourself.

Today, honor your word to yourself and believe in yourself to keep commitments that you made to you. Who will be the integrity keeper in this? That's easy look in the mirror…You!

Today I honor my word to myself

"Nothing is at last sacred but the integrity of your own mind."

~ Ralph Waldo Emerson

Today

I Claim
My Destiny

Today your destiny is waiting for you. Are you ready for it? On this day, say yes to it! Do not be shy or try to hide from your passion and your purpose. The destiny you seek is there for you. Today is your day to claim it, love it, and embrace it.

On this day, show up and show out. Many people wait for their luck. You do not wait for anything; you own your lot in life. You claim your birthright to be great. Today be impassioned about who you are to answer God's call of your greatness.

Your greatness or vocation is to be the best person that you can be in this world. Set your intentions to live out your destiny with purpose and joy.

Today I claim my destiny

"It is not in the stars to hold our destiny but in ourselves."
~ William Shakespeare

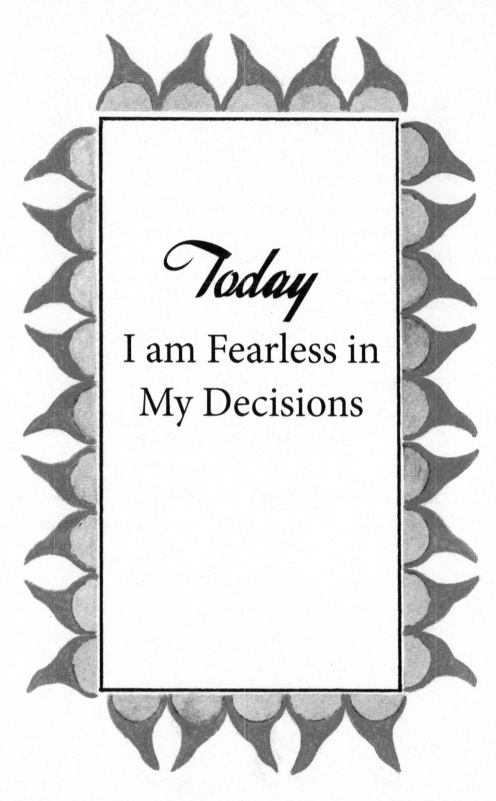

Today

I am Fearless in My Decisions

Today you make decisions without fear. Today you take risks and you are extremely confident that any risk is better than no action.

Decisions held back by fear have a cost. When you allow fear to control your movements, it makes you powerless in thoughts and actions. Today bust through that fear and make choices based on knowledge, gut instinct, and confidence. Spend your energy wisely and be fearless in your decisions.

Today, you know in the moment that every choice you make creates its own set of consequences. From a core level, your confidence is such that you will identify what needs to be done and act upon it.

Build your trust muscle today. Keep your integrity intact, trust yourself and the decisions that you make.

A person who is visionary makes decisions that are powerful. Today you are visionary. You are powerful. You are fearless. You are brave!

Today I am fearless in my decisions

" *The fearless are merely fearless. People who act in spite of their fear are truly brave.*"

~ *James A. LaFond-Lewis*

Today

I Breathe

Today take a deep conscious loving breath. Your breath sustains life and is your key to relieving stress and maintaining a connection with Source.

Today, with every breath you take, allow yourself to float on the air of your breath and acknowledge the presence of life. Your breath sustains your dreams, gives you life, and anchors you to the Divine.

Today take a breath, slowly inhaling in and acknowledging God's presence, and on the exhale releasing the day into God's care. Focus your breath and as you begin this day, breathe in and breathe out. Life is good.

Today I breathe

" Breath is the bridge which connects life to consciousness, which unites your body to your thoughts."

~ Thich Nhat Hanh

Today

My Future
is Bright

Today, be excited for what the future holds. Your future is what you make it and today you are eager and open to the possibilities that await you.

Begin this day in gratitude for being alive and know that anything is possible in your future. Today, strive to live your best life with no hesitation, no judgments and no regrets.

Celebrate life today and make awesome, bodacious plans for your future. Envision life's simplest pleasures and create a future starring you. Stay hopeful, strong, and be confident that you are a positive being of light.

Your future shines brightly. Your dreams that are shimmering in the distance are waiting for you to grab them. Go for it!

Today my future is bright

" *When I look into the future, it's so bright it burns my eyes.*"

~ Oprah Winfrey

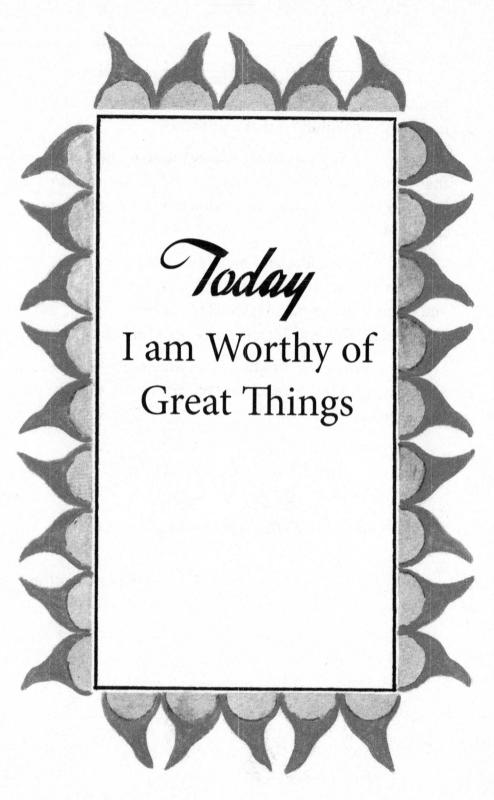

Today

I am Worthy of Great Things

Today you are a child of royalty. Therefore, walk with your head held high. Your stance is proud and you strut like a peacock in full-feathered bloom because you know you are worthy.

From the depths of your soul, you claim your worthiness. Today, you are charged with putting an infinite price on your self-worth. You are worthy of great things; thus you are priceless.

As one of God's priceless objects d'art, treat yourself with care. Walk with purpose and in each interaction that you have with someone let them feel as if every word out of your mouth is golden and every action you take is a priceless nugget. Today, you are worthy of great things… so act like it!

Today I am worthy of great things

" And God blessed them. And God said to them, 'Be fruitful and multiply and fill the earth and subdue it and have dominion over the fish of the sea and over the birds of the heavens and over every living thing that moves on the earth.'"

~ Genesis 1:28

Today

I Am at Peace

Today is a peaceful day for you. You are at peace and you instill peace. Today your environment is tranquil and you move with grace and ease.

Everything you do today comes from a place of calm. Your actions are thoughtfully motivated to bring the highest good to all those involved.

On this day, move throughout the world with quiet purpose and determination. Today fulfill your place on earth as a peacemaker.

Today, all storms roll back as you allow peace to enter into your life and create a safe harbor for yourself and others.

Today I am at Peace

" The LORD gives strength to his people; the LORD blesses his people with peace."

~ Psalm 29:11

Today

I Fly on the
Wings of God

Today, thank God for giving you wings to fly. On this day, look up among the clouds and feel confident in your ability to soar. Today, have no worries about the flight plan. You have absolute faith in the flight planner. Visualize yourself soaring, and as you view the horizon, see the vast possibilities of your life.

Today, with this inflight knowledge, smile and realize you are truly blessed. Today wherever your journey may take you, embark on it with courage and endless joy, as today you fly on the wings of God.

Today I fly on the wings of God

" It is beautiful to discover our wings and learn how to fly; flight is a beautiful process. But then to rest on the wings of God as He flies: this is divine."

~ C. Joybell.C

Today

I Play and
Have Fun

Today make a new rule in your life. Have some fun and remember to play. Life is to be enjoyed. Today there is no shame when you play. Today is a day free of guilt and filled with pleasure and crazy fun. Take delight in the fact that you can live your best life by fully indulging in a bit of play.

Today you are charged with doing what you feel. For some, it might be curling up with a good book, it could be taking the day off for a mental health day, stopping to wiggle your toes in the sand, or even just taking a catnap in the middle of the day. Whatever your pleasure, do something that you enjoy!

Not sure what to do? Ask a child. Better yet, reconnect with your own inner child. Say hello to your childlike self and play.

Today I play and have fun

" We do not cease to play because we grow old; we grow old because we cease to play!"

~ George Bernard Shaw

Today

I Take Action

Today all of your actions are inspired by your goals. Your committed promise today is to take action on your dreams. In other words, just do something.

Begin the day by visualizing your goal. Use the power of creative visualization as a blueprint for your innermost goals. As you visualize the result, and experience the feeling in your mind of what that outcome is to be, you focus the energy on your next steps. This will inspire action and you have a greater chance of achieving your dreams.

Any action you take today is based upon the goals that you have. Have faith in yourself, have faith in your dreams, and take action.

Today I take action

" *Our goals can only be reached through a vehicle of a plan, in which we must fervently believe, and upon which we must vigorously act. There is no other route to success.*"

~ *Pablo Picasso*

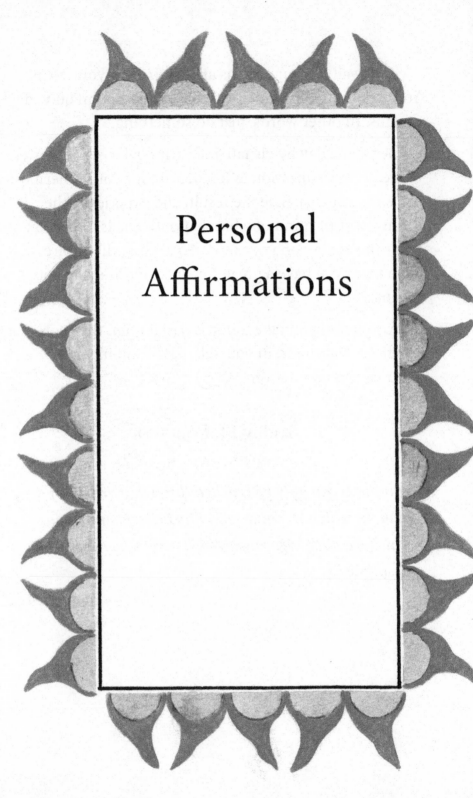

Personal
Affirmations

It is now time to create your own affirmations. Affirmations are effective as they reprogram your mind. It is time to put your abilities to work as you create a new vision for yourself that is impactful and clear.

Create your own powerful affirmations in each category—heart-centered, soul-centered, and mind-centered that sustains your new way of being.

These affirmations work, as they come from your own desires and have the ability to program your mind into believing them to be true. Your mind does not know the difference between what is real or fantasy, so make your affirmations powerful and meaningful as you manifest your destiny.

Soul-Centered

Soul-centered is your connection to the Divine. It matters not what you call it, be it God, Source, the Divine, the Universe, or Goddess, only that you subscribe to the belief that there is something greater than you.

When you believe that there is a more powerful force or that there is the collective spirit of the Universe then you are ready to believe.

This belief allows you to surrender expectations and acknowledge the place in your soul with wonder and delight.

Today

I/My_____

_____

_____

Quote_____

_____

_____

_____

Heart-Centered

To be heart-centered is to be one with you. Our lives are so complex that we are often torn in many different directions and our heads become full of chatter from all the noise and interference of others. In the still, small, quiet space between breath and light is the essence of you.

Today, take a moment to listen intently. In that space of peace and tranquility, allow yourself to hear from your heart. These are your heart-centered moments.

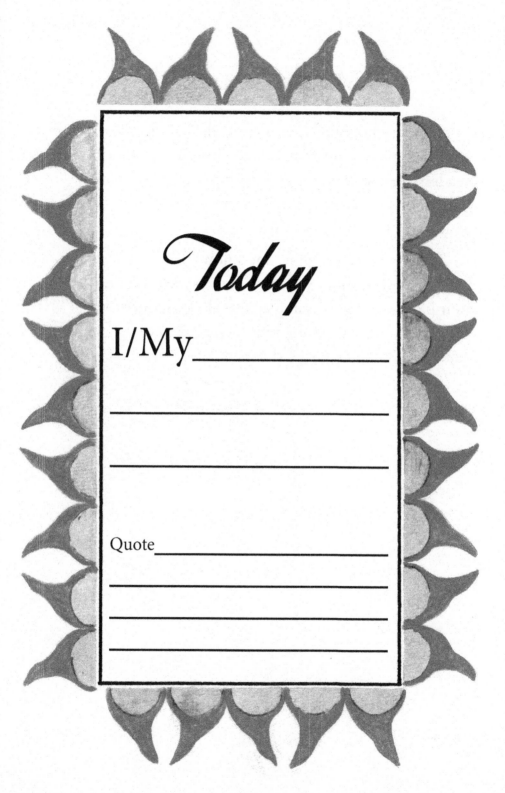

Today

I/My_____

_____

_____

Quote_____

_____

_____

_____

Mind-Centered

A centered mind allows one to take action. When your mind is focused, you take a leadership role in your life. Leaders are constantly in motion and in contemplation. Contemplate what makes the most sense and then act on it.

Today you contemplate and know that there is more to life than following. When you act like a leader in your life, you take risks and accept all consequences. Ultimately, those who are mind-centered have the ability make decisions and to get things done.

Today

I/My_____

_____

_____

Quote_____

_____

_____

_____

Notable Quotes

Quotes are a great way to solidify affirmations. Using quotes helps you to remember that others have walked similar paths. The Biblical quotations are taken from the Old Testament in order to be more inclusive to world religions.

Notable Quotes

Thanks and Praise

Mere words cannot express the love and gratitude that I have for all the many angels who worked with me to turn this book into a reality.

First, last, and always, I give thanks to God and give him the highest praise. I am grateful to the Blessed Mother and to the Archangels Gabriel, Raphael, and Michael. Writing this with guidance from the Divine has given me immeasurable joy.

Many thanks to the Grammar Goddess, Susan Rooks, and my amazing editor Sandra James, as they kept the integrity of my voice while polishing the tone of the book. Also thanks to artist, Jean Maniscalco for her beautiful cover art and book illustrations and to Karen White for artistic layout and graphic design.

Huge shout-out to the members of my Diamond Mastermind Group: Janet, Juliette, Patty, Sheri, Tricia, and Trisha for encouragement and unceasing cheerleading.

To my extraordinary Dream Team of Angela, Bernadette, Darryl, Gloria, and Tawilhua: you all believe in me and support me when I am leaping in faith and for that, I am incredibly thankful.

I am indebted to so many of you not mentioned here who were with me on this journey and I thank you.

Muchísimas Gracias

Sandra

Photo: Tracey Harper

About the Author

Sandra Elaine Scott is a
Life Coach, Corporate Trainer, and
Transformational Speaker.

For more information on Sandra's
speaking, coaching, and
training programs and services
please connect with her at
Sandra@ mananastartstoday, and on
twitter @SandraElaineSco

CPSIA information can be obtained
at www.ICGtesting.com
Printed in the USA
BVOW04s1827090317
478237BV00001B/19/P